# NO BEES, PLEASE!

Story By
**Nicole Serchion Dennis**

Illustrated by Timothy Brooks

Printed in the United States of America

First Printing, 2018

ISBN 978-1-7326042-0-9 (Hardcover Edition)
ISBN 978-1-7326042-1-6 (Digital Edition)

www.LittleScaryMouse.com

Oh my goodness!! Oh no! Oh no!

It is almost spring
and no more snow.

# Time to take off hats and gloves

and to get to wear all the dresses
I love, BUT...

# THE BUGS,
# THE
# BUGS!

I'm so afraid of the bugs!!
They are creepy and crawly and make me all itchy.
I want to be brave like my big cousin Richie.

I run and I scream and
I hide in the house.

My mommy and daddy call me
their little scary mouse.

They tell me "Be still and the bees will buzz by."
No one gets why I even run from butterflies.

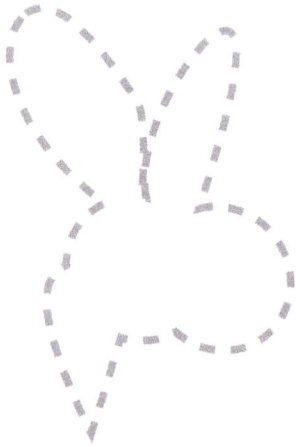

I'm a big girl now, I just turned four.
I don't want to be a scaredy cat anymore.

I want to be outside and see the flowers and trees,
not crouching by the window on my hands and my knees.

Grandma said we wouldn't have flowers if we didn't have bees.
What?? No flowers without buzzing bees?
No pretty blooming and no pretty trees?

So, if I got my wish and they all went away,
spring would be like winter, all gloomy and gray.

I guess bees aren't so bad. I can learn to stand still.

And butterflies and ladybugs can flutter around me, at will.
They aren't trying to hurt me, just happy it's spring.
They wake up from their naps to fly and to sing.

I can do this — be brave and not run away scared.

Oh my, look at the butterfly sitting right there!

The bees aren't chasing, just focused on flowers.
I feel so much better, like a super hero with powers!
I won't miss this spring, won't stay in the house.
And I'm no longer my parents' little scary mouse.

THE END

# NO BEES, PLEASE!

www.ingramcontent.com/pod-product-compliance
Lightning Source LLC
Chambersburg PA
CBHW040253100426
42811CB00011B/1246

9 781732 604209